I0411315

Introduction to PSPP

A Step by Step Guide

Elizabeth Bigham, Ph.D.

Copyright © 2013 Elizabeth Bigham, Ph.D.
All rights reserved.
ISBN-13: 978-1481150880
ISBN-10: 148115088X

DEDICATION

This text, Introduction to PSPP, is dedicated to Rick. Thank you for accepting my little obsessions. ☺

CONTENTS

FORWARD

Health and human services students learning statistics and research methods are often introduced to software programs with incredible capabilities. The cost of the software may be reasonable for businesses but out of the reach for students.

This text goes through the steps of basic set-up and statistical analysis using a free statistical software program called PSPP which can be downloaded for free at http://www.gnu.org/software/pspp/get.html. The program does not have all the whistles and bells of other expensive statistical software programs but it does many analyses and the publishers continue to update it.

If you find PSPP to be useful, please send them your thanks. Their information is included at the end of the book and I, for one, think that it is awesome that they have provided this analysis software for free.

.

1 PREPARING FOR ANALYSIS

This chapter introduces the basic data entry steps to get you started with preparing data for analysis.

Note that the text in this book refers to the sample survey included at the end of the book.

Check the surveys

Start by going through your surveys (if done on paper) or downloaded data (if survey done with an online survey), looking for data that is obviously wrong. For example, someone who indicated that their age is 222. You will need to make some decisions, such as when to remove an entire survey or when to correct the entry, etc. Make notes about any decisions that you make and your reasoning. This is also good time to number your surveys.

Assign a layout

Open PSPP. This opens the PSPPIRE Data Editor. Notice that at the bottom left of your screen there are two tabs (Data View and Variable View). You are currently in Data View which is the screen for entering data - one participant per row, one variable entry per column.

Develop your codefile

Switch to the Variable View: Click on **Variable View**. Variable View is where you define and code your variables. The variables are entered – one per row. It is good practice to use participant number or case as the first variable and then start going through your variables, in the order that they are presented to the participant.

Note: The word "variable," as used here, may be confusing. When you are designing your project, "variable" may refer to a concept like Level of Stress or Heart Rate. Heart Rate would be entered in PSPP as a variable (Name could be HeartRate, for example), however, let's say that you measured Level of Stress with a 5 item Stress Questionnaire. Level of Stress then would be entered on 5 lines, one for each question (Names could be Stress1, Stress2, Stress3, Stress4, Stress5). Thus, the word "variable," as used here, refers to each data item that is collected.

Name

Starting with the Name column, enter *Case* as the first variable (write "Case" in the top cell in the left column). You will notice that the columns to the right of *Case* fill in automatically with default information. We will go through those columns next – but first, continue to enter the variables from the sample survey in the first column. For example, write *Sex* on line 2 in the first column, write *Age* on line 3, *Ethnicity* on line 4, *School* on line 5, *HSGPA* on line 6, *CollegeGPA* on line 7, *Confidence* on line 8, *Control1* on line 9, *Control2* on line 10, *Control3* on line 11, and *Control4* on line 12.

Note: Variable names should be brief but enough that you can identify what it is. Review the sample survey and the list of names above and you will find that there is a variable name here for each place for data in the survey. The last 4 variables represent the 4 questions at the end which are adapted from Burger, J.M. and Cooper, H.M.'s scale measuring desirability of control scale (1979) (similar to the Level of Stress example above). We will put the raw

---

data in for multi-question scales and then tell PSPP how to score it for us.

Type

The Type column's default setting is Numeric data. If this variable is non-numeric data (words that will not be coded at this point, such as responses to open-ended questions), click on the cell and then on the area that is shaded. You can then select the new setting, such as String. You can change the column width and number of decimal places here if you wish. Click **OK**.

Note: Numeric data is preferred for quantitative analysis. It includes data which is numbers (i.e. response to *Age* would be a number) as well as categorical data that has been coded (i.e. response to *Sex* would not be a number but we would code it as 1 = Female, 2 = Male, etc.).

Width and Decimals

You can change the column width and number of decimal places here as well. It is a good idea to change the decimal places for each variable to zero unless you think you'll need it (i.e. money, GPAs, etc.). To change the decimal places, click in the box in the Decimals column on the line you want to change and scroll up or down to the desired number.

Label

The Label column is an area where you can write in the full question or any other information to help you identify the variable. Later, you may want to have the labels on your printouts or have information close to each variable while you are interpreting your results so it pays off to write each question in. To enter the question, click in the box in the Labels column on the line of the variable name that corresponds to the question and type (or cut and paste from your text document) the question.

Values

This is where you tell PSPP what the values are for each of the response options on your survey – when the response options are categorical. For example, *Sex*, your second variable, is categorical (participant's responses will be words for different categories, such as male or female). You need to give each possible response a value, such as 1 = Female, 2 = Male. To enter values, click in the box in the Values column on the line of the variable name that corresponds to the question and then click on the area shaded in grey. A Value Labels window will appear. Enter "1" in the Value box and "Female" in the Value Label box. Select **Add.** Then enter "2" and "Male." Select **Add.** Select **OK.**

> Note: The variables on our sample survey that would be coded include: Sex, Ethnicity, School (1 = community college, 2 = 4-year university 3 = other), Confidence (1 = strongly disagree, 2 = somewhat disagree, 3 = somewhat agree, 4 = strongly agree), Control 1, Control2, Control3, and Control4 (1 = applies to me, 2 = somewhat applies, 3 = never applies). No need to code Age, HSGPA, or CollegeGPA as they are already numeric.

Missing, Columns, Align

We will discuss options for the Missing Column later. Columns and Align are formatting options that you can change if you wish.

Measure

The Measure column is where you indicate the level of measurement of the variable. Choices are Nominal, Ordinal, or Scale (interval or ratio). Click on the cell, then on the down arrow, and make your selection.

> Note: The level of measurement (LoM) here is referring to the LoM of the output data for that variable now, as it is entered on that line (not necessarily the same as after it has been scored or anything else has been done to it).

Enter Data

A sample data set is included on the next page in Table 1 for you to use to go through the rest of the steps covered by this text. While it might be tempting to use your own data set, taking the time to enter and then use this data set will allow you to try each step and check your answers against the ones in the examples.

To get started, go to the Data View spreadsheet by clicking on the **Data View** tab in the bottom left corner of the screen. Start with the first participant by entering the case number in the first row of the *Case* column. For variables that are coded, enter them as numbers (i.e.1 for Female). You can click on **Value Labels** at the top of the page to have the spreadsheet show the words (i.e. Female) instead of the number (i.e. "1").

Note: Leave the cells blank when there is missing data (i.e. a participant does not respond to an item). Later, each analysis will indicate if there is missing data and how many cases were used in each analysis.

Table 1

Sample Data Set

Case	Sex	Age	Ethnicity	School	HighSchoolGPA	College GPA	Confidence	Control 1	Control 2	Control 3	Control 4
1	1	23	1	1	2.9	2.8	1	1	2	3	2
2	2	24	5	2	2.8	3.2	4	2	2	2	2
3	1	25	4	1	3.1	3.4	3	3	1	2	3
4	1	26	2	1	3	3	2	3	1	1	2
5	1	24	3	3	2.8	3	2	3	2	2	1
6	2	25	5	3	2.9	3.1	3	2	3	2	2
7	1	26	4	3	2.9	3	4	2	3	2	3
8	1	22	2	1	2.6	3.3	2	1	2	1	2
9	2	56	6	2	2.7	3.5	1	2	1	1	1
10	2	47	1	2	2.8	3.2	.	2	2	2	1
11	1	36	5	1	3.1	3	3	2	3	3	2
12	2	25	2	3	2.7	3	4	1	2	3	3
13	2	36	4	2	2.6	3	4	1	2	2	3
14	2	24	4	2	2.3	3.1	3	2	2	1	3
15	2	34	1	3	2.9	3.4	2	3	3	2	2
16	1	40	.	1	3	3.4	3	3	2	3	2
17	1	25	1	1	2.8	2.8	2	2	1	2	1
18	2	26	1	2	2.9	3.1	1	1	2	2	2
19	1	24	2	1	2.5	2.5	2	2	3	2	2
20	1	25	3	3	3	3	2	3	2	3	2
21	2	26	2	3	2.4	2.7	3	2	1	2	1
22	1	22	4	3	3.2	3.2	4	2	1	1	1
23	1	56	1	1	3.1	3.5	3	2	2	2	2
24	2	47	1	2	2.7	3	3	3	3	3	3
25	2	36	4	2	2.9	3.4	2	2	3	2	3
26	2	25	5	2	2.8	3.1	2	1	3	1	2
27	2	36	6	3	2.4	3	1	2	2	1	1
28	1	24	4	3	2.9	3.1	2	3	2	2	2
29	2	34	4	2	2.8	3.4	3	2	1	3	3
30	1	40	6	1	2.5	2.8	4	1	2	3	2

Check your entries

Once you have entered your data, it is important to check carefully for errors. You can enter the data twice and have the computer compare the two datasets. You could run descriptive statistics on all your variables and verify that the minimum and maximum values for each variable do not exceed the possible value range for that variable (e.g., if you find your maximum value for Sex is 33, you know there is a problem). Also, examine the standard deviation and sample size for all variables. You may want to make a scatter plot or a histogram to check for outliers or normality.

ELIZABETH BIGHAM, PH.D.

2 WORKING WITH VARIABLES

This chapter covers several of the steps of working with variables, including scoring, using a sample data set. Keep in mind that these are the basic steps that you will need to adapt to your specific data set as each is unique.

Add a variable

To add a variable in Data View, **Left click** on the grey portion at the top of the column of the variable to the right of where you want to add the variable. **Right click**. Select **Insert variable** (or click the Insert Variable button at the top of the page).

Note: You can double Left click on the new temporary variable name in Data View to quickly switch to Variable View to give the variable a name. Use the Add a Case button next to the Add a Variable button in the same way to add a Case.

Remember to save your file frequently.

Note: From here on, you will end up with two PSPP files open at a time. PSPP will open an output file that shows what you have done (i.e. what you recode in the next steps, any analyses that you carry out, etc.). Therefore, it is important to remember to save often AND that you have 2 files open thus 2 files to save (one is the data file and the other is the output file). You can click on the icon in the lower left of your screen to switch back and forth.

Combine Variables

Sometimes you want to combine responses, either because scoring instructions instruct you to do so or because you want to compare groups in a specific way. For example, the *Confidence* variable has participants' responses to the statement "On the whole, I am satisfied with myself." To make a comparison of the participants who "agreed" (strongly agree and somewhat agree) and those who "disagreed" (strongly disagree and somewhat disagree), you can combine the two "agree" answers and the two "disagree" answers so that there are only two categories of answers to the statement, instead of 4.

For this example, you would:

1. Select **Transform**. Select **Recode**. Select **Into Different Variables**. In the window called *Recode into Different Variables,* highlight the variable you want to recode (i.e., *Confidence*), click on the small arrow to move this variable into the *Variables* box.

> Note: By choosing Recode "Into Different Variables," we told PSPP to leave the original data intact – just use the data to make a new column with our new coding. If you choose the other Recode option (Into Same Variables), PSPP overwrite the old data with the newly coded data. This may sound tempting but most of the time it leads to trouble as your original data is now gone. Recode Into Different Variables will make a new column for the newly created variable and it will be at the bottom if you are looking in Variable View or at the far right if you are looking in Data View.

2. Name the new variable by typing its title in *Output Variable: Name* (i.e. *Confidence2*). Click on the **Change** button.

3. Click on **Old and New Values**.

4. Type in the old value in the *Old Value: Value* box. This can be a single number or a range of numbers. Notice several options below the Value box.

5. Type in the new value in the *New Value: Value* box.

6. Click on **Add**. Repeat these steps until all values are included in the Old New box.

7. Click on **Continue.** Then **OK.**

Note: For this example, we will recode *Confidence* from 1 = strongly disagree, 2 = somewhat disagree, 3 = somewhat agree, 4 = strongly agree into a Different Variable called *Confidence2* with 1 = strongly disagree or somewhat disagree, 2 = somewhat agree or strongly agree. To make all the 1s and 2s into 1s and all the 3s and 4s into 2s, enter "1" in the *Old Value: Value* box and "1" in the *New Value: Value* box; enter "2" in the *Old Value: Value* box and "1" in the *New Value: Value* box; enter "3" in the *Old Value: Value* box and "2" in the *New Value: Value* box; enter "4" in the *Old Value: Value* box and "2" in the *New Value: Value* box.

Reverse Scoring

Use the same procedure that you used to combine variables (above) to reverse score variables. For example, the scoring instructions for the Control measure in the sample survey (the last 4 questions) said to reverse score Control question #3 then add up all the responses.

Note: If the scoring instructions say to reverse score several questions, you can do them all at the same time if they have the same number of response options.

For the reverse scoring portion of those instructions in this example, you would:

1. Select **Transform**. Select **Recode**. Select **Into Different Variables**. In the window called *Recode into Different Variables,* highlight the variable you want to recode (i.e., *Control3*), click on the small arrow to move this variable into the *Variables* box.

2. Name the new variable by typing its title in *Output Variable: Name* (i.e. *Control3Reversed).* Click on the **Change** button.

3. Click on **Old and New Values**.

4. Type in the old value in the *Old Value: Value* box.

5. Type in the new value in the *New Value: Value* box.

6. Click on **Add**. Repeat these steps until all values are included in the Old New box.

7. Click on **Continue.** Then **OK.**

Note: For this example, we would recode Control3 from 1 = applies to me, 2 = somewhat applies, 3 = never applies to Control3Reversed with 3 = applies to me, 2 = somewhat applies, 1 = never applies. To make all the 1s into 3s, 2s into 2s, and 3s into 1, enter "1" in the *Old Value: Value* box and "3" in the *New Value: Value* box; enter "2" in the *Old Value: Value* box and "2" in the *New Value: Value* box; enter "3" in the *Old Value: Value* box and "1" in the *New Value: Value* box.

Using formulas to create new variables

You can transform existing variables mathematically to create new variables. For example, you may want to combine the participant's high school and college GPAs into one average GPA. To do this:

Steps to create a new variable:

1. Select **Transform**. Select **Compute**.

2. Start building a formula by highlighting the first variable of your formula and moving it to the *Numeric Expression* box by clicking on the right arrow (i.e. *HighSchoolGPA*). Click on the calculation that you want to perform and this will place it in the formula (i.e. "+"). Highlight the next variable in your formula and move it to the *Numeric Expression* box (i.e. *CollegeGPA*).

3. Complete the formula by typing parentheses before HighSchoolGPA and after CollegeGPA. Enter a "/" and "2" so that the formula looks like this: (HighsSchoolGPA+CollegeGpa)/2

5. Type the name of your new variable in the *Target Variable* box (i.e. *AverageGPA*).

6. Click on **OK**.

Note: In the Reverse Scoring example, the scoring instructions for the Control measure in the sample survey (the last 4 questions) said to reverse score Control question #3 then add up all the responses. You can use the Compute command to do the second part of those instructions (add up all the responses.) To do this, select **Transform**. Select **Compute**. Highlight and move *Control1*, then click "+", then *Control2*, then click "+", then *Control3Reversed*, then click "+", then Control4, then "+". Formula should look like this: *Control1 + Control2 + Control3Reversed + Control4.*

Create a Subset

You may want to create a subset of participants to analyze, such as only those who attended Community College. Use this command if you only want to analyze participants that meet specific criteria. The other data will not be deleted but will not be used in the next analyses. Be sure to remove the filter if you decide that you no longer want to restrict your analysis to those you selected for your subset.

Steps to create a subset:

1. Select Data. Select Cases.

2. Check *Use filter variable*

3. Highlight variable (i.e. School) and click on the arrow to move it to the box

4. Click **OK**.

Generate a data dictionary

It is very handy to have a printout of your data dictionary in front of you when you are doing your analyses. It is a listing of each variable that you created, how you coded each one (i.e. 1 = females, etc.), and other choices you made when you defined it in PSPP.

Steps to create a data dictionary:

Select **File**. Select **Display Data File Information**. Select **Working File**.

Your data dictionary will appear as an output window that you can download or print.

See the sample portion of the data dictionary in Table 2 on the next page.

Table 2

Sample Data Dictionary

Variable	Description	Values	Position
Case	Format: F2.0 Measure: Scale Display Alignment: Right Display Width: 8		1
Sex	Format: F1.0 Measure: Scale Display Alignment: Right Display Width: 8 1 2	 female male	2
Age	Format: F2.0 Measure: Scale Display Alignment: Right Display Width: 8		3
Ethnicity	Format: F1.0 Measure: Scale Display Alignment: Right Display Width: 8		4
School	Format: F1.0 Measure: Scale Display Alignment: Right Display Width: 8 1 2 3	 Community College 4-year University Other	5

3: Descriptive Statistics

This chapter covers how to produce a summary of the distribution of scores. You should know these concepts:

- Levels of Measurement (Nominal, Ordinal, Interval, Ratio)
- Measures of Central Tendency (Mean, Mode, Median)
- Measures of Dispersion (Standard Deviation, Range)

If these are a bit fuzzy for you, you should review them in a statistics text before doing this Chapter. There are also many great explanations available online, just be sure to check that it is from a reputable source.

Reporting variables

Descriptive statistics summarize data. If you will be doing inferential statistics, it is good practice to present descriptive statistics first to provide a context for your reader, including who was in the study (Demographics), how your participants performed on your measures (Descriptive Statistics), etc.

Start by describing your sample. Include the number of participants, their ages, sexes, ethnicities, etc., and any other variables that are important in illustrating how they represent the population of interest.

Nominal and Ordinal variables, such as type of school (from our sample survey), are reported as Frequencies, either as percent or number in each category. Interval and Ratio variables, such as High School GPA, are typically reported as the range of scores obtained, skewness, average score, and standard deviation.

Nominal and Ordinal Variables

Sex, for example, would be reported as percent in each category (___% males and ___% females, as measured on the sample survey). To calculate Frequencies for nominal and ordinal variables, perform the following steps:

1. Go to **Analyze**. Select **Descriptive Statistics**. Select **Frequencies** from the *Data View* or *Variable View* menu bar.

2. Move your variables to the Variables box by highlighting and clicking on the arrow.

3. Select **Frequency Tables** to review settings and make sure it is set to do Frequency Tables.

4. Then **Continue**. Select **OK.**

Review the sample output in Figure 1: Use the first table which shows the frequency of each level of each variable, such as percent of females and males. You would ignore the second table as you would not report means and standard deviations for nominal and ordinal variables.

In this example, 50% of the participants were females and 50% were males.

```
FREQUENCIES

FREQUENCIES
    /VARIABLES= Sex
    /FORMAT=AVALUE TABLE.
```

Sex

Value Label	Value	Frequency	Percent	Valid Percent	Cum Percent
	1	15	50.00	50.00	50.00
	2	15	50.00	50.00	100.00
Total		30	100.0	100.0	

Sex

N	Valid	30
	Missing	0
Mean		1.50
Std Dev		.51
Minimum		1.00
Maximum		2.00

Figure 1. Frequencies output displays percentages used to report nominal and ordinal variables.

Interval and Ratio Variables

Age, for example, would be reported with a range (youngest to oldest age in the study), average age, and standard deviation, as follows: "Participants' ages ranged from 22 to 56 years old with an average age of 31.3 (*SD*=9.87)." High School GPAs would be reported as "High School GPAs ranged from 2.29 to 3.23 out of a possible 0 to 4.0. The distribution was negatively skewed (-.53) with an average score of 2.803 (*SD*=.22)." To calculate Minimum, Maximum, Mean, Skewness, and Standard Deviation for interval and ratio variables, perform the following steps:

1. Go to **Analyze**. Select **Descriptive Statistics**. Select **Frequencies** from the *Data View* or *Variable View* menu bar.

2. Move your variables to the Variables box by highlighting and clicking on the arrow.

3. In the **Statistics** box, check **mean, standard deviation, skewness, minimum** and **maximum**.

4. Optional: Select **Charts** and choose a chart.

5. Then **Continue**. Select **OK.**

Review the sample output in Figures 2 and 3. The first table shows the frequency of each level of each variable (i.e. % who had each GPA level). For interval and scale variables, you would focus on the second table as it lists the mean, standard deviation, skew, minimum, and maximum.

In this example, participants ages ranged from 22 to 56 years old with an average age of 31.3 (SD=9.87). See Figure 3.

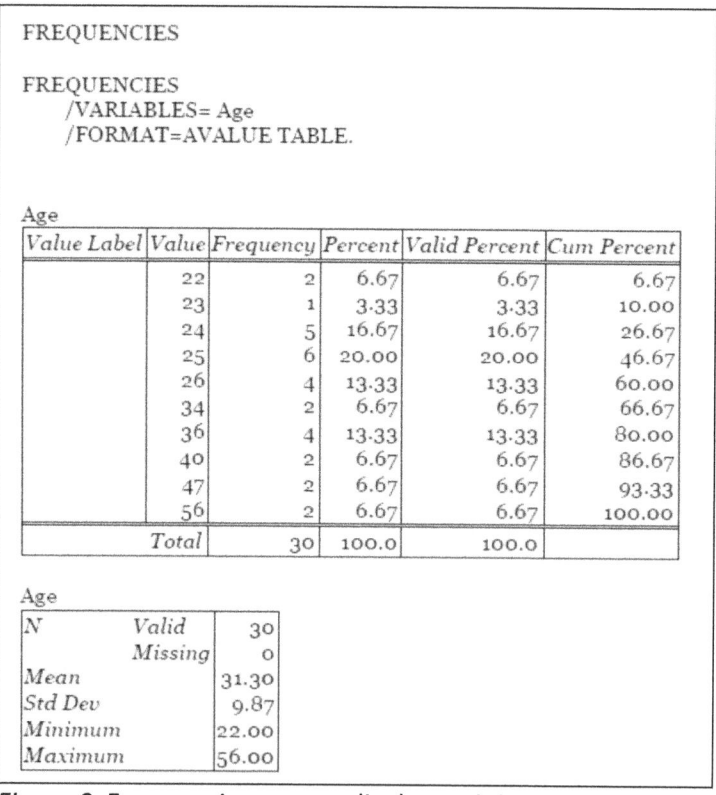

FREQUENCIES

FREQUENCIES
    /VARIABLES= Age
    /FORMAT=AVALUE TABLE.

Age

Value Label	Value	Frequency	Percent	Valid Percent	Cum Percent
	22	2	6.67	6.67	6.67
	23	1	3.33	3.33	10.00
	24	5	16.67	16.67	26.67
	25	6	20.00	20.00	46.67
	26	4	13.33	13.33	60.00
	34	2	6.67	6.67	66.67
	36	4	13.33	13.33	80.00
	40	2	6.67	6.67	86.67
	47	2	6.67	6.67	93.33
	56	2	6.67	6.67	100.00
Total		30	100.0	100.0	

Age

N	Valid	30
	Missing	0
Mean		31.30
Std Dev		9.87
Minimum		22.00
Maximum		56.00

Figure 2. Frequencies output displays minimum, maximum, mean, and standard deviation to report scale variables.

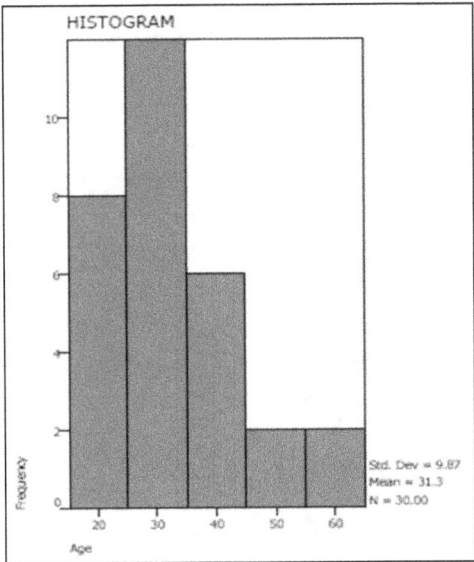

Figure 3. Histograms and other charts can be used to illustrate important findings.

Transferring to your document
Tables and graphs in PSPP are not in APA format. You might want to use a spreadsheet software program as it is usually easier to format Tables and Graphs into APA format there than in a text software program. You can export output in CSV format then open in your spreadsheet software program. Whatever strategy you use, be sure to save your files so you can go back to them and make corrections.

ELIZABETH BIGHAM, PH.D.

4: Which Analysis?

This chapter reviews the steps of hypothesis testing, features of a good hypothesis, and how to decide which analysis to do, in general terms.

Recall the steps of analysis

You should know the 5 steps (actions) of analysis (remember this from statistics class?):

Action 1. Review the details of your study

What is/are your hypothesis(es)? What are the variables? Which are IVs? Which are DVs? What is the level of measurement of the resultant data? If nominal or ordinal, how many levels or groups? Are they within or between?

Action 2. Select a significance level

Typically .05 or .01 (.05 means that, if the findings are less than .05, chances are less than 5 in 100 that the findings are not true (very unlikely that the null is true), so we reject the null. If you need to be surer of your findings (say in the case of a drug that has harmful side effects), you may want to choose a lower significance level to reduce the chance of making a Type I error (rejecting the null when in fact the null was true). If you need to be surer that you don't miss a finding, you may want to choose a higher significance level to reduce the chance of making a Type II error (not rejecting the null when the null is false).

Select: One-tailed or Two-tailed (Does your hypothesis predict that the difference or relationship between the variables will be in a specific direction?)

Action 3. Determine which analysis and perform the analysis

Are you examining group differences, strength of relationship, etc.? Use the **Decision Tree** below to help you with this step.

Action 4. Determine significance

After calculating in PSPP, review the results to determine if you have any significant findings (any with levels of probability that are smaller than the p-value you chose).

Action 5. Decide

Decide whether you will reject or fail to reject the null hypothesis.

A "Good" Hypothesis

A well written hypothesis can make a big difference in how confident you are about your study's design and analysis. While the overall study objective is often broad and conceptual, the hypothesis should have specific variables and a clear, precise prediction of the relationship between those variables (a defined population as well).

For example:
Let's say you have noticed that many of the clients who are served by your unemployment agency seem to be very stressed about their financial situation while other clients seem to not be stressed. Your initial interviews with the clients leads you to believe that relationships with other family members is the reason – clients in families with healthy relationships are better able to cope with change due to losing their job. Do you propose a general hypothesis with the two variables (underlines):

> "Family relationships affect the amount of stress suffered by clients who are unemployed."

This is a good general hypothesis, but it does not specifically state the direction of the relationship. Here it is reworded so that the direction (underlined) is clear.

> "Clients who are unemployed suffer less stress when family relationships are healthier."

The hypothesis now clearly states the proposed direction but it is still a bit abstract (what component of healthy?). Here it is reworded again with some clarification (that healthy, in this case, is cohesiveness) that will help the researcher to know exactly what to measure and test (underlined).

> "Clients who are unemployed suffer less stress when family relationships are healthier because they are more connected to their family members."

This is a testable hypothesis – it has specific variables and a clear, precise prediction of the relationship between those variables (and a defined population as well).

Decision Tree I

It is important to have a solid understanding of your design, hypotheses, and planned analyses before you collect any data. Even so, you may find that you need to re-acquaint yourself with your own study by the time you are ready to do your analysis.

Ask yourself, what did I want to know more about when I designed this study? For example, "I wanted to know if a person's personality anxiety (trait not state) profile is related to how they deal with stress (mind and body)." This is your study objective.

Best bet is to draw out a model of your design indicating the manipulations, relationships, proposed directions, whether measures are between or within, etc. for the overall research question/objective and then identify each hypothesis.

Now think through your analysis (below), one hypothesis at a time.

1. What is your hypothesis?

Hypothesis:

_____

_____

For example, anxiety is related to psychophysiological stress, such that increases in trait anxiety levels will be related to increases in resting heart rate.

2. What are the variables that you used in this hypothesis?

Variables:

_____

_____

For example, the variables from this example are trait anxiety (as indicated by score on anxiety scale) and psychophysiological stress (as indicated by heart rate).

3. Which variables are IVs and which are DVs (their role in this hypothesis only)?

IVs:

_____

_____

DVs:

_____

_____

For example, IV: trait anxiety (score on anxiety scale) DV: psychophysiological stress (heart rate)

Note: Recall that the Independent Variable (IV) is the presumed cause of change of your Dependent Variable (DV). One way to get it straight is to try your variables in both positions of this statement and see which makes sense: "_____ (IV) is the presumed cause of change of _____(DV)."

For example, "trait anxiety (IV) is the presumed cause of change of psychophysiological stress (DV)" makes sense whereas "psychophysiological stress (IV) is the presumed cause of change of trait anxiety (DV) could make sense but would be a different study, not consistent with the key question for this study.

Another way to help get it straight is to think about time in that if the IV is the potential cause of change, it has to occur (in time) before the DV.

For example, if you want to know if _trait anxiety_ is related to _psychophysiological stress,_ you would know that _trait anxiety_ is the

IV because it is presumed to be formed in childhood which would be before the other variable, *psychophysiological stress,* which is how their body is currently functioning.

4. What type of measurement is your dependent variable?

Nominal   Ordinal   Scale

Remember that this is asking about the resultant data, not the individual questions. Also, keep in mind that this is a general basic decision tree to get you started.

For example, if you had a 10 question *trait anxiety* scale that was scored into a total *trait anxiety* score, the total *trait anxiety* score would be the resultant data and it would be **scale**. If you measured *heart rate* as a one item indicator of *psychophysiological stress*, the *heart rate* would be the resultant data and it would also be **scale**.

On the other hand, if you asked participants what situation makes their heart rate go up the most (i.e. taking a test, asking for a raise, speaking in front of a group, thinking about the future), then your resultant data is **nominal**. You would then need to determine (for nominal or ordinal data) how many levels or groups? For this example, it would be 4 groups (taking a test, asking for a raise, speaking in front of a group, thinking about the future).

5. If your answer to #4 was:

Nominal or Ordinal, how many variables do you have? _____

If 1, Chi Square Goodness of Fit (compare your sample to a known sample)

If 2, Chi Square Test of Independence (for example, 2 nominal variables)

<<<You are done with the Decision Tree for this hypothesis.>>

Scale, how many (nominal/ordinal) IVs do you have? _____

    If 0, how many DVs? _____

    If 1, is the population known? _____

       If yes, z test

       If no, t test single mean

    If 2 or more, are you examining relationship or predicting? _____

       If relationship, correlation

       If predicting, regression

If 1, how many levels? _____

    If 2, are they between (i.e. different people in different groups) or within (i.e. .same people measured more than once)?

       If between, t test for independent samples

       If within, t test for dependent samples (also called matched, pairs, or repeated)

    If 2 or more, One way ANOVA

If 2 or more, for each IV – is it between (i.e. different people in different groups) or within (same people measured more than once)? _____

There are several different types of ANOVAs and other analyses from this point. You might consult your statistics textbook or review on online review from a reputable source.

5: Crosstabs & Chi-Square

This chapter covers how to produce a summary of the distribution of the relationship of scores and test whether the relationship is significant with a chi-square analysis using the sample data.

Distribution of Multiple Variables

To determine the frequency of a combination of variables, such as how many of each *Sex* were from each type of *School*, use Crosstabs. To run a Crosstabs for multiple nominal or ordinal variables, perform the following steps:

1. Go to **Analyze**. Select **Descriptive Statistics**. Select **Crosstabs** from the *Data View* or *Variable View* menu bar.

2. Move one variable to the *Row* box by highlighting it and clicking on the arrow.

3. Move the other variable to the *Column* box by highlighting it and clicking on the arrow.

4. Select **Cells** and check *count, rows, columns, and total*

5. Then **Continue**. Select **OK.**

Review the sample output in Figure 4: The first table summarizes the number of cases used and missing. Focus on the second table which has output in rows (levels of one variable) and columns (levels of the other variable). It shows the frequency of each level of each variable (i.e. how many of each *Sex* were from each type of *School*).

The Crosstabs table can be difficult to read at first. You can download the output as a csv file and open it in your spreadsheet software program (in case you want to highlight or delete some items). This is what I have done for the next example in Table 3. It is the same data as is in the middle box of the Crosstabs above – just shaded in to make it easier to talk about the sections of the spreadsheet. Notice that each box in Table 1 has 4 numbers. These represent the *count, rows, columns, and total* that you checked when you performed the Crosstabs. You can get a lot of information out of this table.

In this example, reading across by row (light shade), this shows that the 66.7% of the females took their lower division courses at a Community College, 0% at a 4 Year University, and 33.3% at another location while 0% of the males took them at a Community College, 56.7% at a 4 Year University, and 33.3% at another location. Reading down by column (darker shade), it shows that the 100% of the Community College students were females and 0% were males; 0% of the 4 Year University students were females and 100% were males; and 50% of the Other location students were females and 50% were males. Reading this one just looking at totals (bold items), it shows 33.3% of the students were Females from Community College, 16.7% were Females from Other, 33.3% were Males from 4 Year University, and 16.7% were Males from Other.

```
CROSSTABS

CROSSTABS
    /TABLES= Sex  BY  School
    /FORMAT=AVALUE TABLES PIVOT
    /CELLS=COUNT ROW COLUMN TOTAL.
```

Summary.

	Cases					
	Valid		Missing		Total	
	N	Percent	N	Percent	N	Percent
Sex * School	30	100.0%	0	0.0%	30	100.0%

Sex * School [count, row %, column %, total %].

Sex	School			Total
	1	2	3	
1	10.00	.00	5.00	15.00
	66.67%	.00%	33.33%	100.00%
	100.00%	.00%	50.00%	50.00%
	33.33%	.00%	16.67%	50.00%
2	.00	10.00	5.00	15.00
	.00%	66.67%	33.33%	100.00%
	.00%	100.00%	50.00%	50.00%
	.00%	33.33%	16.67%	50.00%
Total	10.00	10.00	10.00	30.00
	33.33%	33.33%	33.33%	100.00%
	100.00%	100.00%	100.00%	100.00%
	33.33%	33.33%	33.33%	100.00%

Figure 4. Crosstabs output shows frequencies of more than one variable.

Table 3

Distribution of Participants by Sex and Lower Division Setting

Sex	Community College	4 Year University	Other	Total
Female	10	0	5	15
	66.70%	0.00%	33.30%	100.00%
	100.00%	0.00%	50.00%	50.00%
	33.30%	0.00%	16.70%	50.00%
Male	0	10	5	15
	0.00%	66.70%	33.30%	100.00%
	0.00%	100.00%	50.00%	50.00%
	0.00%	33.30%	16.70%	50.00%
Total	10	10	10	30
	33.30%	33.30%	33.30%	100.00%
	100.00%	100.00%	100.00%	100.00%
	33.30%	33.30%	33.30%	100.00%

Chi-square

A Chi-Square analyzes the relationship between variables in two ways: 1.) "Goodness of fit" (rarely used in research) which compares expected and observed frequencies of one nominal variable with several categories. A significant result would indicate that there is a significant deviation from the hypothesized values; and 2.) The "test for independence" which analyzes the relationship between nominal variables (usually two, each with several categories).

For example, Chi-Square Test for Independence can be used to determine if there is a significant relationship between Gender and type of School. PSPP has Chi-Square in Crosstabs and Non-parametric tests.

To perform a Chi-Square in Crosstabs, perform the following steps:

1. Go to Analyze > Descriptive Statistics > Crosstabs from the Data View or Variable View menu bar.
2. Move one variable to the Row box by highlighting it and clicking on the arrow.
3. Move the other variable to the Column box by highlighting it and clicking on the arrow.
4. Select Statistics and check Chisq (Chi-Square). Then Continue
5. Select Cells and check count, rows, columns, and total
6. Then Continue > OK.

Review the sample output in Figure 5: The first two tables are the same as in the Crosstabs. The first table summarizes the number of cases used and missing and the second table output is in rows (levels of one variable) by columns (levels of the other variable) and shows frequency of each level of each variable (i.e. how many of each Gender were from each type of School). The third table shows the results of the Chi-Square analysis of whether the variables are related to (dependent on) each other.

In this example, "A 2 (Sex) x 3 (School) chi-square analysis was used to examine whether gender was related to type of school attended for lower division undergraduate work. The analysis was significant, $X^2(2, N = 30) = 20.00, p < .01$." This means that the distribution of different sexes (males and females) was different at different types of schools (community college, 4 year university, and other).

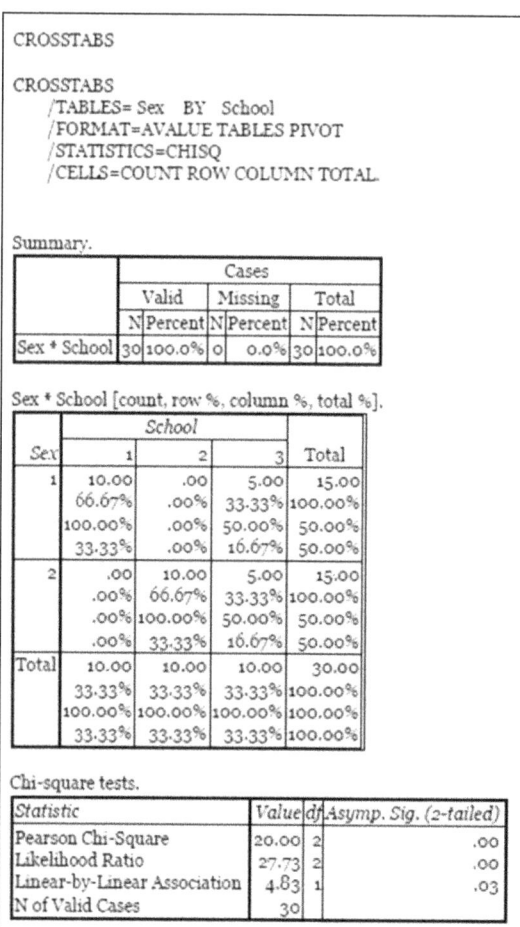

Figure 5. Chi-Square output is displayed below the Crosstabs.

6: Correlation & Regression

This chapter reviews the steps of running a correlation and regression using the sample data.

Note: Remember to save your files now and then.

Correlation

A Pearson correlation analyzes relationships between parametric, linear (interval, ratio, "scale" in PSPP) variables. If ordinal, use Spearman Rho even if not from a normal distribution. You can enter several variables and get a matrix of the relationships (direction and strength, -1 to 1).

1. In Data View or Variable View, go to **Analyze**. Select **Bivariate Correlation**.

2. Click on one of your variables in the list of variables in the left box and then click on the arrow button to move it to the right box.

3. Then click on your other variable(s) and move it into the right box.

4. Check **Two or One-tailed** and **Flag significant correlations**.

5. Then click **OK**.

Review the sample output in Figure 6: While you can put several scale variables into the correlation at once, each bivariate analysis is of the relationship between 2 variables. Find the box where the 2 variables intersect (1 variable across the top and the other down the side). Each box has a correlation value, significance (p-value), and N.

In this example, "There was a positive correlation between high school GPA and college GPA, r (30) = .42, p = .01, one tailed." Square the correlation value (to calculate r2) as this will give you the percent of the variation of one variable that is related to the variation in the other. In this case, it would only be 17.64%, meaning that only 17.64% of the change in high school GPA can be accounted for by change in college GPA.

CORRELATIONS

CORRELATION
    /VARIABLES = HighSchoolGPA CollegeGPA
    /PRINT = ONETAIL NOSIG.

Correlations

		HighSchoolGPA	CollegeGPA
HighSchoolGPA	Pearson Correlation	1.00	.42
	Sig. (1-tailed)		.01
	N	30	30
CollegeGPA	Pearson Correlation	.42	1.00
	Sig. (1-tailed)	.01	
	N	30	30

Figure 6. Correlation matrixes display the relationship between variables.

Regression

Regression investigates whether level on one variable can be predicted by knowing the level on the other variable. For example, We want to know if we can predict College GPA by knowing a person's High School GPA.

Simple linear regression is used for two interval/ratio variables with a normal distribution (some exceptions apply). Multiple regression is used to predict a level of a variable using two or more predictor variables.

1. From **Analyze**, choose **Regression.** Choose **Linear**.

2. Move the variable that you are trying to predict to Dependent.

3. Move the variable(s) that you are trying to predict from to Independent.

4. Click **OK**.

Review the sample output in Figure 7: The first table is the Model Summary which shows the R value (absolute value of correlation coefficient), R Square (proportion of the variation of the dependent variable that can be explained by the independent variable) and Std. Error of the Estimate (standard deviation of the confidence intervals). The second table, ANOVA, is where you check for significance (is it less than .05?). The third table, Coefficients, in column B, the constant is the intercept and the variable is the slope.

Regression results are often reported in a table that shows the regression coefficient for each predictor variable and the overall R or R2.

In this example, "Linear regression analysis was used to test if the *high school GPAs* significantly predicted *college GPAs*. The results of the regression indicates 18% of the variance in *College PGA* can be explained by differences in levels of *High School GPA*, $F(1,29)=6.17$, $p=.02$)."

The regression equation would be: College GPA = 1.79 + (.47 * High School GPA).

REGRESSION

REGRESSION
   /VARIABLES= HighSchoolGPA
   /DEPENDENT= CollegeGPA
   /STATISTICS=COEFF R ANOVA.

Model Summary (CollegeGPA)

R	R Square	Adjusted R Square	Std. Error of the Estimate
.42	.18	.18	.23

ANOVA (CollegeGPA)

	Sum of Squares	df	Mean Square	F	Significance
Regression	.32	1	.32	6.17	.02
Residual	1.46	28	.05		
Total	1.78	29			

Coefficients (CollegeGPA)

	B	Std. Error	Beta	t	Significance
(Constant)	1.79	.53	.00	3.38	.00
HighSchoolGPA	.47	.19	.42	2.48	.02

Figure 7. Regression outputs include information for the regression equation.

7: *t* Test & ANOVA

This chapter reviews the steps of running simple group comparisons.

t Test

A *t* Test compares differences on an interval/ratio variable in three different formats

Single Sample *t* Test

A Single Sample *t* Test compares the average of a sample to the known population average. For example, you could compare the *High School GPAs* of the sample population to a published freshman class average (Average GPA = 3.0). To run a single sample t test, perform the following steps:

1. Click on **Analyze**. Select **Compare Means**. Select **One Sample *t* Test.**

2. Move the variable that you want to compare to the population average into the Test *variable* box. (for this example, move *High School GPA*)

3. Enter the population average in the Test *value* box. (for this example, use "3.0")

4. Click on **OK.**

Review the sample output in Figure 8: The first box has the number of participants in the analysis, mean and standard deviation of the sample. The second box has the results of the comparison.

In this example, "Participants in the study had lower high school GPAs (*M*=2.80, *SD*=.22) than the published freshman class average, *t*(29) = -4.78, *p* < .01.

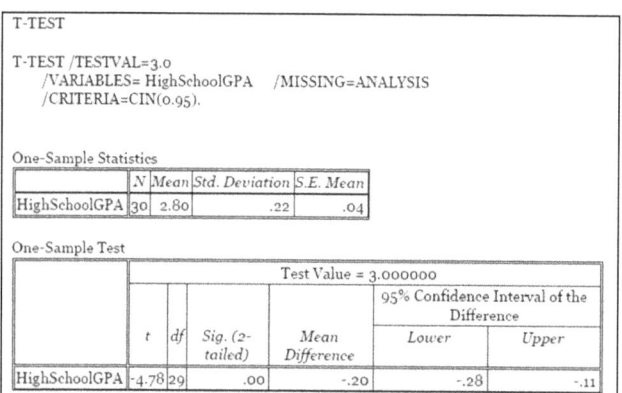

Figure 8. T Test for Single Sample output shows how the population's average compared to the test value/average.

Independent Samples *t* Test

An Independent Samples *t* Test compares the differences between two independent samples. For example, you could compare Confidence levels of Males and Females.

1. Click on **Analyze**. Select **Compare Means**. Select **Independent Samples *t* Test.**

2. Move the variable that defines the two groups that you are comparing to the *Define Groups* box (for this example, move *Sex*)

3. Click on the **Define Groups** tab and define what two groups you will be comparing (for this example, you would enter "1" for Females and "2" for Males). Click **Continue.**

4. Move the dependent variable you want to test to the *Test Variable(s)* box (for this example, move Confidence).

5. Click on **OK**.

> Note: You can also compare two groups out of a larger number of groups. For example, you could compare participants who went to Community College to those who went to 4 Year University. You would put *School* in the Define Groups box and under the Define Groups tab, you would enter "1" and "3".

Review the sample output in Figure 9: The first box shows mean and standard deviation for each group used in this analysis.

The second table shows the Levene's Test, followed by the t Test. If the Levene's is not significant, you can assume equality of variances and use the top line of the t Test results. If the Levene's is significant, you cannot assume equality of variances so use the bottom line of the t Test results.

In this example, "No significant difference was revealed between Males' Confidence (N = 14, M = 2.57, SD = 1.09) and Females' Confidence (N = 15, M = 2.60, SD = .91); $t(27)$ = .08, p =.94, two-tailed.

T-TEST

```
T-TEST /VARIABLES= Confidence
       /GROUPS=Sex(1,2) /MISSING=ANALYSIS
       /CRITERIA=CIN(0.95).
```

Group Statistics

	Sex	N	Mean	Std. Deviation	S.E. Mean
Confidence	1	15	2.60	.91	.24
	2	14	2.57	1.09	.29

Independent Samples Test

	Levene's Test for Equality of Variances		t-test for Equality of Means					95% Confidence Interval of the Difference	
	F	Sig.	t	df	Sig. (2-tailed)	Mean Difference	Std. Error Difference	Lower	Upper
Confidence Equal variances assumed	.66	.42	.08	27.00	.94	.03	.37	-.74	.80
Equal variances not assumed			.08	25.43	.94	.03	.37	-.74	.80

Figure 9. T Test for Independent Samples output shows the comparison of two groups.

Paired (Dependent) Samples t Test

A Paired Samples *t* Test compares the differences between two dependent (paired) samples, such as pre and post measures of the same person. For example you could examine change in GPA from high school to college.

Note: In some of the analyses (including this one), the pop up window in PSPP is too small to see what you are doing. So it is a good idea to enlarge the analysis box when it pops up.

1. Click on **Analyze**. Select **Compare Means**. Select **Paired Samples *t* Test.**

2. Click the first variable (i.e. high school GPA) then click the arrow. See it appear under Var1.

3. Click on the second variable (i.e. college GPA) then click the arrow. See it appear under Var2.

4. Click on **OK.**

Review the sample output in Figure 10: The first box shows the mean and standard deviations for the variables. The second box shows the correlation of the paired samples. The t Test results are in the third box.

In this example, "Participants' college GPAs (*M*=3.10, *SD*=.25) were significantly higher than their high school GPAs (*M*=3.1, *SD*=.22), *t*(29)= -6.39, *p*<.01, two tailed."

```
T-TEST

T-TEST
    PAIRS = HighSchoolGPA WITH CollegeGPA (PAIRED)
    /MISSING=ANALYSIS
    /CRITERIA=CIN(0.95).
```

Paired Sample Statistics

	Mean	N	Std. Deviation	S.E. Mean
Pair 0 HighSchoolGPA	2.80	30	.22	.04
CollegeGPA	3.10	30	.25	.05

Paired Samples Correlations

	N	Correlation	Sig.
Pair 0 HighSchoolGPA & CollegeGPA	30	.42	.02

Paired Samples Test

	Paired Differences							
				95% Confidence Interval of the Difference				
	Mean	Std. Deviation	Std. Error Mean	Lower	Upper	t	df	Sig. (2-tailed)
Pair 0 HighSchoolGPA - CollegeGPA	-.30	.25	.05	-.39	-.20	-6.39	29	.00

Figure 10. T Test for Paired Samples output shows the comparison of two related scores.

ANOVA

An ANOVA (*F* Test) compares differences between groups on interval/ratio variable(s). The analysis focuses on variances as it is analyzing how several means differ (the variation among the means) and, if more than one independent variable, it also analyzes the interaction (the special effect of the combination of the variables). If your findings are significant, you need to do additional (planned) comparisons to determine which means are significantly different.

First, you need to determine which type of ANOVA you need to do (see discussion in Chapter 4).

Identify your variables.

Determine which are independent variables (IVs) and which are dependent variables (DVs) in this analysis.

Determine each variable's level of measurement (nominal, ordinal, interval, ratio).

Determine if this analysis has within subjects or between subjects comparisons or a combination.

Note: Your variables' roles in this analysis are often different that they have been in another of your analyses. One example is that they can be an IV in some of your analyses and a DV in others. Another example is that they could be individual variables in that are put together as one variable. For example, in our sample study, we measured GPA twice (once for high school, once for college) so these two together can be analyzed as a within subjects variable.

Run a One-Way ANOVA:

If you have one independent variable and you are comparing independent (between subjects) groups, do a One-Way ANOVA. For example, you could compare *College GPA* and *Confidence* levels in participants who had different types of *School* for lower division coursework.

1. Click on **Analyze**. Select **Compare Means**. Select **One Way ANOVA.**

2. Move your dependent variable(s) to the *Dependent* box (for this example, *College GPA* and *Confidence*).

3. Move your independent variable (defines your groups) to the *Factor* box (for this example, *School*).

4. Check **Descriptive.**

5. Select **OK.**

Review the sample output in Figure 11. The first table shows the means and standard deviations for each School group for each DV (College GPA and Confidence). The second table has the results of your ANOVA.

In this example, "No significant differences were revealed in college GPAs between participants from Community College (M=3.05, SD=.34), 4 Year University (M=3.19, SD=.18), and Other (M=3.06, SD=.18), F(2, 29) = 1.09, p = .35. No significant differences were revealed in Confidence levels between participants from Community College (M=2.50, SD=.85), 4 Year University (M=2.56, SD=1.13), and Other (M=2.70, SD=1.06), F(2, 28) = .10, p = .90."

```
ONEWAY

ONEWAY /VARIABLES= CollegeGPA Confidence BY School
     /STATISTICS=DESCRIPTIVES .
```

Descriptives

		N	Mean	Std. Deviation	Std. Error	95% Confidence Interval for Mean		Minimum	Maximum
						Lower Bound	Upper Bound		
CollegeGPA	1	10	3.05	.34	.11	2.81	3.29	2.5	3.5
	2	10	3.19	.18	.06	3.06	3.32	3.0	3.5
	3	10	3.06	.18	.06	2.93	3.19	2.7	3.4
	Total	30	3.10	.25	.05	3.01	3.19	2.5	3.5
Confidence	1	10	2.50	.85	.27	1.89	3.11	1	4
	2	9	2.56	1.13	.38	1.69	3.42	1	4
	3	10	2.70	1.06	.33	1.94	3.46	1	4
	Total	29	2.59	.98	.18	2.21	2.96	1	4

ANOVA

		Sum of Squares	df	Mean Square	F	Significance
CollegeGPA	Between Groups	.13	2	.07	1.09	.35
	Within Groups	1.64	27	.06		
	Total	1.78	29			
Confidence	Between Groups	.21	2	.11	.10	.90
	Within Groups	26.82	26	1.03		
	Total	27.03	28			

Figure 11. ANOVA output shows the comparison of two or more groups.

It is a good practice to calculate estimated power during the design phase of your study. You should calculate it again during analysis if you have non-significant findings. There are several good power analysis tools available for free online.

More ANOVAs

This may be where PSPP becomes quite limited compared to the more expensive commercially produced programs, however, they are expanding and regularly doing updates.

If you have one independent variable and you are comparing correlated (within subjects) groups, do a Repeated Measures ANOVA. If you have two or more independent variables and you are comparing independent (between subjects) groups for all variables, do a Factorial ANOVA. If you are comparing correlated (within subjects) groups for all variables, do a Repeated Measures ANOVA. If you have a combination of independent and correlated group comparisons, do a Mixed Design ANOVA. These seem to be beyond the scope of PSPP so you will need to purchase another statistical software package for these analyses.

Also, with multiple comparisons, you need to conduct contrasts and post-hoc tests. Again, you will probably need to purchase another statistical software package for these analyses.

Appendix

PSPP Sample Survey

Please respond to the following items.

What is your sex?   Male   Female

What is your age?   _____

What is your race/ethnicity?   _____

Where did you complete your first 2 years of college units?
Community College   4-Year University   Other

What was your high school GPA (n/a if not
applicable)?   _____

What was your college GPA (n/a if not applicable)?   _____

How much do you disagree/agree with the following statement:
            Overall, I knew I would be successful in college.

Strongly Disagree	Somewhat Disagree	Somewhat Agree	Strongly Agree

How often do the following statements apply to you?*
1=applies to me,   2=sometimes applies,   3=never applies

___ I enjoy being able to influence others regarding their finances.

___ I am careful to check every possible option before I make a

___ Others usually know what financial planning strategy is best for me.

___ I enjoy making my own decisions about my finances.

*Adapted from Burger, J. M., & Cooper, H. M. (1979). The desirability of
control. Motivation and Emotion, 3, 381 393.*

CLOSING

As an instructor, I want these instructions to be as clear and accurate as possible. Please send your comments, reactions, favorite statistics limerick, etc. to: ebigham@csusm.edu.

www.ingramcontent.com/pod-product-compliance
Lightning Source LLC
Chambersburg PA
CBHW070622290526
45790CB00002B/958